COCO CHANEL BIOGRAPHY BOOK

By David Right

ALL COPYRIGHTS RESERVED 2017

All Rights Reserved

Copyright 2017 by David Right - All rights reserved.

This document is geared towards providing exact and reliable information in regards to the topic and issue covered. The publication is sold with the idea that the publisher is not required to render accounting, officially permitted, or otherwise, qualified services. If advice is necessary, legal or professional, a practiced individual in the profession should be ordered.

- From a Declaration of Principles which was accepted and approved equally by a Committee of the American Bar Association and a Committee of Publishers and Associations.

In no way is it legal to reproduce, duplicate, or transmit any part of this document in either electronic means or in printed format. Recording of this publication is strictly prohibited and any storage of this document is not allowed unless with written permission from the publisher. All rights reserved.

The information provided herein is stated to be truthful and consistent, in that any liability, in terms of inattention or otherwise, by any usage or abuse of any policies, processes, or directions contained within is the solitary and utter responsibility of the recipient reader. Under no circumstances will any legal responsibility or blame be held against the publisher for any reparation, damages, or monetary loss due to the information herein, either directly or indirectly.

Respective authors own all copyrights not held by the publisher.

The information herein is offered for informational purposes solely, and is universal as so. The presentation of the information is without contract or any type of guarantee assurance.

The trademarks that are used are without any consent, and the publication of the trademark is without permission or backing by the trademark owner. All trademarks and brands within this book are for clarifying purposes only and are the owned by the owners themselves, not affiliated with this document.

PREFACE

The brand Chanel is known and loved by people of all age groups since a very long time. Since the very inception of the brand, Chanel has been one of the most sought after fashion houses of the world, and is more or less like the leader in the fashion world. From established fashion designers to the girl next door who just likes to dress up her prettiest best, everyone has some or the other connection to Chanel. They all follow Chanel, learn from Chanel, and take inspiration from Chanel in a way or the other.

Today, Chanel is not only a name that signifies class, perfection, style, elegance and divine, pure and elite fashion, but it is in fact the outcome of a fashion revolution started by Coco Chanel, the designer who changed the way fashion designers thought and executed their ideas. In 1957, Coco Chanel proved to be the Queen of the fashion world when she became the recipient of the Neiman Marcus Fashion Award.

Chanel's greatest creations are considered to be her classic Chanel 2.55 handbag and some fragrances and clothes which were her brainchildren. The Chanel 2.55 handbag revolution-alized the way handbags were designed for women and Chanel was the first to propose the idea that handbags should be made in such a way that they free women's hands, and are comfortable to carry. Plus, the variety that she brought in with the different sizes meant that women of all kinds could carry these bags on all sorts of occasions, whether they are formal or casual.

From its initial days to the present times, Chanel has come a long way, adding more and more feathers to its hat. A number of celebrities have been spotted over the years carrying Chanel bags or walking down the ramp for Chanel fashion shows. More celebrities have been part of the ad campaigns that have been brought out by Chanel for their clothes and fragrances.

Table of Contents

BIOGRAPHY OF COCO CHANEL BOOK 1

ALL COPYRIGHTS RESERVED 2017 2

PREFACE 3

    CHAPTER 1- THE BIOGRAPHY OF COCO CHANEL 6

    The First Glory of Chanel 8

    The Birth of Chanel No. 5 Perfume 10

    CHAPTER 2 – COCO CHANEL SECRETS TO CLASSIC INFLUENCE 19

    COCO CHANEL STYLES 21

    CHAPTER 3- COCO CHANEL AND THE HOUSE OF CHANEL 24

    THE HOUSE CHANEL 25

    CHAPTER 4- THE INVENTIONS OF COCO CHANEL THAT CHANGED THE FASHION WORLD 28

    THE LITTLE BLACK DRESS 28

    TROUSERS FOR WOMEN 29

    THE INTRODUCTION OF JERSEY 29

    THE 2.55 HANDBAG 30

    THE BRAID-TRIMMED BOUCLE COLLARLESS JACKET 30

    DESIGNER PERFUME 30

    COSTUME JEWELLERY AND FAUX PEARLS 31

    SAILOR TOPS 31

    THE CHANEL SUIT 32

    THE CHANEL TWO-TWO PUMP 32

    CHANEL'S PERFUMES- WHAT MAKES CHANEL SO DESIRABLE 33

    THE HISTORY OF THE LITTLE BLACK DRESS 36

    CHAPTER 5- THINGS YOU DID NOT KNOW ABOUT COCO CHANEL 38

    CHAPTER 6- CONCLUSION 42

Gabrielle Coco Chanel..42

THE CHANEL HOUSE 48

CHAPTER 1- THE BIOGRAPHY OF COCO CHANEL

Coco Chanel (1883 – 1971) is an outstanding French fashion designer, creator of the fashion empire of the XX century. She is the founder of The House of Chanel. Her net worth is $15 billion. Her real name is Gabrielle Chanel.

"Fashion is what one wears oneself. What is unfashionable is what other people wear", this is the famous quotation from Oscar Wilde. It was disproved by Coco Chanel in the mid-20s of the previous century who stated that fashion was the "little black dress". Her authority was so great that women from different social classes unhesitatingly were wearing Chanel clothing.

Early Life, Career and First Love

Gabrielle was born on August 19, 1883, in Saumur, France in the family of fair trader Albert Chanel and his girlfriend Eugénie Jeanne Devolle. He married Jeanne Deville several years after Coco Chanel was born. They did not have a permanent place to live. If things went well, they allowed themselves to have a primitive farm and settled down in some old abandoned shack, which people tried to get round. Her mother was a laundrywoman, in the charity hospital owned by the Sisters of Providence and her father was a street vendor who sold haberdashery goods on the street market.

The legendary Mademoiselle Chanel had been shy of her miserable childhood all her life. She was afraid that reporters could find out about her extramarital origins, her mother's death from bronchitis at the age of 31 or about her father who simply gave up having passed Gabrielle in a shelter at the age of 12. Coco Chanel even invented her story that when her mother died, her father sailed for America, and she lived in a cozy and clean house with two strict aunts, who in reality did not exist.

If you were born without wings, do nothing to prevent them from growing. – Coco Chanel

Having learned sewing arts during her six years at Aubazine shelter, Coco Chanel was able to find a job as a seamstress. When not plying her trade with a needle and thread, she was singing in a cabaret "La Rotonde" fre☐uented by cavalry officers. There Gabrielle acquired her nickname "Coco". It is derived from the famous song "Qui Qu'a Vu Coco?" that she used to sing.

In her early twenties, Coco Chanel concluded that the main thing in life was money. In 1905, when a young and wealthy bourgeois Étienne Balsan came into her life, Coco Chanel hung around his neck. In her eyes, he was the real man, who had money and was able to spend them easily. When she settled in the castle of her lover, Coco took full advantages of her new life. She was lying in bed until noon, drinking coffee with milk and reading cheap novels. However, Étienne did not think Coco was the woman, which was worth spending big money on.

In the spring of 1908, Coco Chanel met with a friend of Balsan Captain, Arthur Edward "Boy" Capel CBE, an English polo player with a straight black hair and a dull complexion. Arthur Capel advised Coco to open a vending hat shop and promised her financial support. Later on, he will become her partner in business and personal life.

Coco Chanel and Étienne Balsan

However, she was obliged to Étienne Balsan, who helped to start her career. Étienne wanted to involve his bothered girlfriend into any matter that under the pretext to evict her from his castle. Coco settled in his bachelor apartment on the Malesherbes Boulevard in Paris where he usually had fun with his girlfriends. It was the place where Coco began making and selling her hats. An interesting fact is that all the former mistresses of Étienne became the first clients of Mademoiselle Chanel. They also expanded the range of her clients to their friends. Things went very well, and soon this bachelor apartment became too small.

The First Glory of Chanel

At the end of 1910, Coco Chanel finally broke up with Étienne Balsan and began to live with Captain "Boy" Capel. In 1910, Coco became a licensed modiste (hat maker) and opened a boutique named Chanel Modes on 21 Rue Cambon in Paris. Soon the street became known throughout the world and had been linked to her name for half a century.

In 1913, Coco Chanel opened her boutique in Deauville that quickly attracted regular clients. The creator of the famous hats dreamt of developing her own line of women's clothing. At this time, she had no right to make a 'real' women's dresses, as she could be brought to justice for illegal competition because she was not a licensed dressmaker. Coco found the solution. She started sewing dresses of jersey fabric, which had been only used for men's underwear and earned her first capital on it. Coco Chanel's close family members have always been supportive. One was her sister, Antoinette Chanel and her aunt, Adrienne Chanel. Both of the girls Coco recruited to model Chanel's designs and advertise the Chanel fashion clothes.

All of her dress-discoveries were born that way. While designing Coco did not excel herself, but simplified details. She did not draw her sketches of clothing and did not sew them. Usually, Coco threw a cloth on a mannequin, then cut and slaughtered a shapeless mass of material until the desired silhouette was manifested.

Chanel quickly became the world fashion designer, turning over the spotlight. She created a style that had been previously unthinkable for women – tracksuits. She dared to appear in the sailor suit and tight skirt on the beaches of seaside resorts. The style produced by The House of Chanel was simple, practical and elegant. However, in 1914, the World War I began. There were chaos and the 'feast during the plague' in France. Coco continued to work vigorously, presenting new demands for clothing and generating new ideas: the first female skinny suit from Chanel. A couple of years later, she sewed a redingote without a belt and ornaments, removing the bust and curves with almost masculine stringency. She created an understated waist, dress shirt, pants for women and beach pajamas.

In order to be irreplaceacle, one must always be different. – Coco Chanel

Despite the fact that The House of Chanel introduced the fashion women's pants, Coco wore them quite rarely, as she believed that a woman would never look in the pants as good as a man would. However, she liked a short man's hairstyle. The reason is simple – short hair is easier to take care of. Once Coco cut her hair and proudly walked out into the world, explaining that everything in her house caught on fire, and it burned her curls. Therefore, in 1917, a trend for short man's hairstyle among women was prevalent. Before the Coco Chanel's action, women had to be longhaired.

In 1919, when her beloved Arthur "Boy" Capel died in a car accident, Coco Chanel said: "Either I die as well. Or I finish what we started together." If this tragedy had not happened in the life of Chanel, she would have never started experimenting with black cloth. Some people say that she brought black color clothes into vogue to make all women in France mourning for her beloved. Coco was not allowed to mourn officially, as she was not married to Arthur Capel.

The Birth of Chanel No. 5 Perfume

In the summer of the 1920s, Coco Chanel opened a big fashion house in Biarritz. Later on, she met with a Russian émigré, the Grand Duke Dmitri Pavlovich, and they both felt the mutual passion to each other. The romance was short but fruitful. Coco learned many new ideas from her exotic lover. How could she forget his stories about the treasures of the Muscovite tsar or the luxury of ecclesiastical vestments? Moreover, after this meeting, there were parts of the Russian folk costume shirts with original embroidery in her new collection. The most momentous is that during the road tour in France, Dmitri Pavlovich introduced Coco to a Russian perfumer, Ernest Beaux, when they stopped in Grasse town. Ernest's father had worked for many years at the imperial court.

The meeting was fruitful for both of them. After a year of hard work and long-term experiments, Ernest placed before of Coco ten samples and divided them into two groups. The first half Ernest Beaux numbered from one through five, the second one – from twenty through twenty-four. Coco chose the sample No. 5 and when Beaux asked her why Coco Chanel replied: "I always launch my collection on the 5th day of the 5th months, so the number 5 seems to bring me luck – therefore, I will name it No. 5".

The marketing policy of The House Of Chanel was targeted to celebrities. This choice was not accidental: in the list of clients who wore Chanel No. 5 perfume were the most beautiful women of the century. Chanel No. 5 was a favorite perfume of Jacqueline Kennedy. However unwittingly, Marilyn Monroe invaluably promoted "Chanel". Moreover, she did it free. In the early 1950s, in one of the interviews, Marilyn said that all she wore in bed was a few drops of Chanel No. 5 perfume. A few days later her statement skyrocketed sales of Chanel No. 5 perfume.

Designers spilled the golden liquid into a crystal bottle with a modest rectangular label that looked to them a peculiar solution; usually, perfume bottles had intricate shapes. As a result, the world had a 'perfume for women that smelt like a woman'. It was the first synthetic perfume of eighty components that were not repeating the smell of a particular flower, as it had been earlier. The success experienced its creators – Chanel No. 5 is still the best-selling perfume in the world.

A woman who doesn't wear perfume has no future. – Coco Chanel

The Little Black Dress

By the early 20s, the world almost ended up in fighting for gender inequality. Women had a legal right to work, to vote and to make abortion, but at the same time, they lost their face. Fashion was going through a situation where due to the sad egalitarianism women's clothing began to lose its sexiness and sophistication.

Coco Chanel got this point and successfully managed to combine incredible details in her models with revolutionary innovations and defiant femininity. She invented the famous "little black dress", which seemed, at first, glance, artless, rustic garb and impersonal. This decisive step brought the 44-year designer worldwide fame and made her finding a symbol of elegance, luxury, and good taste.

The first models of the dresses were made of forgotten fluid crepe marocain, knee-length, straight cut with narrow sleeves to the wrists. An incredibly accurate, adjusted and revolutionary cutting length of skirts distinguished them from other ones. By the way, Coco Chanel believed that the bottom of the dress had not to be lifted above the knee because not all women could boast flawless beauty of this part of the body. Cocktail dresses that were more expensive had V-shaped notches and evening dresses had a profound neckline at the back. It was supposed to wear long strings of pearls or colored jewelry, boas, little jackets and tiny hats with such types of dresses.

The little black dress quickly became a cult clothing and acquired a status symbol. It had been often copied, redesigned and retailored. A set of companies and fashion houses still produce this dress around the world. The popularity of this dress is incredible. New interpretations of this dress appear until nowadays so that we can confidently say that this dress will never go out of style.

A girl should be two things: classy and fabulous. – Coco Chanel

While exploring Coco Chanel biography, we learned that in her early 20's, she got involved in jewelry design. The idea to mix crystals and natural stones in a single product came not only to her. However, she was the first who gave life to this idea. Coco actively communicated with the world of Parisian bohemia. She visited ballet performances met with the artist Pablo Picasso, the famous ballet impresario Sergei Diaghilev, the composer Igor Stravinsky, the poet Pierre Reverdy and the playwright Jean Cocteau. Many famous people sought to communicate with the well-known fashion designer just out of curiosity and were surprised to find Coco intelligent, witty and original thinking woman. Once Picasso called her the most sensible woman in the world.

Not only Coco's appearance attracted men but also her extraordinary personal qualities, strong character, and unpredictable behavior. Coco was irresistibly flirty, extremely sharp, straightforward and even cynical. She looked purposeful, confident, contented and successful woman.

Love Affair with Hugh Grosvenor

Later on, Hugh Richard Arthur Grosvenor, 2nd Duke of Westminster, GCVO, DSO (familiarly "Bendor") came into the life of Coco Chanel. He was a British landowner and one of the richest men in the world. Their love affair had lasted for 14 years. This unusually long love affair led Coco into a different environment – the world of British aristocracy.

From 1926 to 1930, the Duke of Westminster was her most welcomed guest. She believed all along that their love would be crowned with marriage. Coco saw the long-awaited final refuge in each of the houses where the Duke took her. They often left England and traveled on his yachts. Usually, Hugh Grosvenor invited about sixty guests on weekends in his estate. Among them, there were Winston Churchill, his wife and close friends of the Duke. They had dinners with live musical accompaniment and sometimes he even invited a theater from London.

Sir Winston Churchill did not hide his enthusiastic impressions, he admired Gabrielle "Coco" Chanel and considered her of the most intelligent, nice and very strong women, with whom he has ever had to deal with.

The well-known politician and statesman, not in vain called attention to these personality traits of Coco Chanel such as determination, willpower, and desire for independence: they brought her to international success.

If she had given birth to the heir of the Duke, she would have become his wife. Prior to 1928, while the passion was strong in him, he was willing to marry her too. Coco was 46 years old when she began visiting doctors, but it was too late – nature opposed to her dream. The Duke of Westminster, suffered no less than his beloved woman but was forced to marry another one.

Coco Chanel's head went back to work. The success accompanied her in all endeavors. She was in the zenith of her fame, and despite her age, (she was already over 50), men found her very attractive.

A Ten-Year Pause in Fashion Career

In 1939, despite the enormous success of her fashion clothing, Coco was forced to close all her shops and the House of Fashion due to the World War II. Many designers left the country, but Coco left in Paris. In September 1944, on the initiative of the Committee on Public Morals Coco Chanel were arrested. The reason was a love affair of Gabrielle "Coco" Chanel with a Walther Friedrich Schellenberg, German SS-

Brigadeführer.Few hours after her detention, she was released. Shortly after that, Coco Chanel moved to Switzerland, where she has lived for almost ten years.

After World War II, designers appeared like mushrooms after the rain in postwar France. One of them, a young fashion designer Christian Dior commented about Coco Chanel's design: "With a black pullover and ten rows of pearls she revolutionized fashion."

Return to the Fashion World

After the war, Christian Dior dressed up women like flowers. He dressed them in crinoline, tightened their waist and filled numerous folds on the thighs. Coco Chanel was laughing at this 'hyper-femininity': "Look how ridiculous these women are, wearing clothes by a man who doesn't know women, never had one, and dreams of being one."

When Coco Chanel returned from Switzerland to Paris, it was full of a generation of fashionistas, who were convinced that "Chanel" is a brand of perfumes. She rented a small two-room apartment at her favorite hotel Ritz in Paris.

Coco got involved in the fashion industry again. When Marlene Dietrich asked Coco Chanel, why she needed it, she explained it her that she was dying of boredom.

The first reaction of experts and press to a new collection of Coco Chanel was shock and outrage – she could not offer anything new! Alas, the critics failed to understand that this was precisely the secret of her: nothing new, only an eternal, timeless elegance. Coco took revenge for a year. The collection that failed miserably in Paris was slightly revised and shown overseas. Americans gave her an ovation. There was a triumph of the little black dress in the United States. It was an honor to a new generation of fashionable women to wear Chanel clothes and Coco herself turned into a tycoon, managing the largest fashion house in the world fashion industry.

During these years, she created the Pink Chanel suit. On November 22, 1963, when the President John F. Kennedy was assassinated his wife wore a double-breasted, strawberry pink and navy trim collared Chanel wool suit. In the 1960s, the Pink Chanel suit has become a symbol for her husband's assassination and one of the iconic items of fashion. Many times the suit has been shamelessly copied to the last braid, to the last golden button and stitching. Nevertheless, the name of Coco Chanel is more than a suit.

Once Coco Chanel said: "Fashion fades, only style remains the same."

The world has recognized her as the only trendsetter of the most refined elegance. The Chanel's style concept firmly anchored in the fashion industry. The Chanel's style means that a suit should be functional and comfortable. If a Chanel suit has buttons, they certainly should be buttoned. A Chanel suit is usually worn with low-heeled toe cross strap shoes. Chanel designed skirt below the knee with pockets where a businesswoman could put a cigarette case. By the way, the idea of wearing a bag over shoulder also belongs to Mademoiselle Coco.

Coco Chanel maintained an incredible performance until old age. New fashion ideas came to her mind even in her sleep. The secret of success of this fantastic brand lies in its roots. From the very beginning,

The House of Chanel sold the art of living but not only clothing for women.

Coco Chanel could not die during a working time. She could not let this happen. On January 10, 1971, she died quietly in the hotel room of Ritz with a window view of the luxuriously decorated The House of Chanel. As of 2014, the revenue of Chanel reached $7.43 billion. When Coco Chanel died, there were found only three dresses in her wardrobe. However, they were "very stylish attires" as would have said Gabrielle "Coco" Chanel.

Legacy

In 1969, Chanel's fascinating life story became the basis for the Broadway musical Coco, starring Katharine Hepburn as the legendary designer. Alan Jay Lerner wrote the book and lyrics for the show's song while Andre Prévin composed the music. Cecil Beaton handled the set and costume design for the production. The show received seven Tony Award nominations, and Beaton won for Best Costume Design and René Auberjono is for Best Featured Actor.

She never married, having once said "I never wanted to weigh more heavily on a man than a bird." Hundreds crowded together at the Church of the Madeleine to bid farewell to the fashion icon. In tribute, many of the mourners wore Chanel suits.

A little more than a decade after her death, designer Karl Lagerfeld took the reins at her company to continue the Chanel legacy. Today her namesake company is held privately by the Wertheimer family and continues to thrive, believed to generate hundreds of millions in sales each year.

CHAPTER 2 – COCO CHANEL SECRETS TO CLASSIC INFLUENCE

Coco Chanel not only created the fashionable and immortal suit and "little black dress" but she made women believe that they can live their own lives, they can be independent and wear clothes according to their own preferences. So powerful was Coco Chanel's influence that today, a bottle of Chanel No. 5 is sold every 30 seconds. Now, that's influence!

Coco set out to conquer the world. She showed women they could be comfortable and still look elegant. Famous for her saying, "In order to be irreplaceable one must always be different," This became Coco Chanel's secret of influence to women everywhere.

What do your clothes say about you?

Is it the right message? Does it work for or against you? What influences your choice of wardrobe? How do you use the power of your clothes?

Your answers to these questions are valuable in making an impression - influencing an outcome - or persuading a thought.

Women in positions of influence, from Wall Street to Washington, face the fashion police every day. For this women fashion and clothing, choices are serious business. But is it any less important for the Mompreneur or the woman teaching third graders? No.

Choosing the right clothes for your personality and the situation is one thing you have control over. Make a note of the clothes you have in your closet. Seriously, go through your wardrobe answering these three questions: How do I feel in this? (not only comfort-wise but emotionally). What am i expressing when I wear this? (try it on then stand in front of the mirror). And, finally, is it me?

Now, here's the key - the answers to these questions should support each other - at least be in tune. If not, it's time to drop it off at good-will, then go shopping!

Women are scrutinized very differently than men. No surprise!

Carly Fiorina, author of "Tough Choices," writes, "while being interviewed by an editor at Business Week during her first month as chief executive of technology at Hewlett-Packard, the first questioned asked, (even though HP was in the midst of a major technology revolution) was, 'Is that an Armani suit you're wearing?'"

Now, I ask you - who in their right mind would think her clothes takes precedence over her solutions for a massive technology upheaval? Would an editor ask Bill Clinton, are you wearing Givenchy, while in the middle of peace talks?

The spotlight on women's clothes and style echoes people's uneasiness in coming to terms with women who have real power. Your image evokes emotions - in others. Even though you see with your eyes, the actual impression or image is perceived by your mind.

For instance, Tony Kornheiser sparked outrage when he told the world, Hannah Storm, 47, was too old to wear flashy red go-go boots, a short skirt, and a top that was 'so tight that she looked like she was wrapped in sausage casing.' Yes, he had a major emotional outburst and was suspended by ESPN for two weeks.

So, what are the unwritten clothing rules for women at work?

- attractive but not tempting
- feminine but not girly
- strong but not harsh

Hmmm... I wonder who wrote these rules?

While it may be true that what you wear doesn't define you as a person, what you wear is a expression of who you are, so choose wisely.

When you choose your next outfit, think carefully about what you wish to tell others, about your mood, your personality, and your ambitions.

Here's the secret to classic influence, "Whatever bait you use determines the type of fish you'll catch."

Coco, see what you started?

COCO CHANEL STYLES

- Form Follows Function

Chanel was a pioneer of a postwar, modern aesthetic for women in the 1920s that embraced comfort and freedom in silhouettes over the restrictive corsets and petticoats. "Luxury must be comfortable," she said, and her designs utilized typical menswear shapes and materials, such as jersey, to achieve this. Chanel looked beyond the mannequin and saw the real woman who would be wearing her clothes.

- The Little Black Dress as Wardrobe Staple

Hailed as one of her most enduring contributions to fashion, the little black frock was a wardrobe essential for Chanel. She considered the garment functional for daytime, evening and anything in between, and today, no modern woman's closet is complete without at least one LBD.

- An Impeccable Tweed Suit Suits Everything

The understated elegance of a Chanel suit never falls out of style—Vogue editor Anna Wintour famously wore them through her pregnancies by unzipping the skirt a bit. The classic collarless boxy jacket and matching skirt were tweaked and updated countless times by Chanel for more than 50 years, ensuring that the look remained relevant.

- Liberate Yourself from the Tyranny of a Clutch

Clutches, which you had to hold in your hands, and wristlets were popular purse styles in the first half the twentieth century. Chanel favored ease of movement instead, and she designed the now-iconic quilted handbag with a chain strap that allowed its wearer to move about hands-free. Known as the 2.55, for its creation in February 1955, the bag has become a status symbol for 'It' girls and practical working women alike.

- Costume Jewelry Can Be Just as Fun as the Real Thing

Chanel was a proponent of wearing fake jewels as much or more than expensive, authentic baubles, famously stating, "It's disgusting to walk around with millions around the neck because one happens to be rich." She became known for piling on strands of pearls and chains as part of a self-styled uniform, making costume jewelry just as covetous as fine jewelry.

CHAPTER 3- COCO CHANEL AND THE HOUSE OF CHANEL

Have you had the pleasure of watching Coco avant Chanel - the story of Coco Chanel's rise from humble beginnings to the heights of the fashion world?

A woman of ambition and determination, Gabrielle Chanel, nicknamed "Coco," rose from humble beginnings and an unhappy childhood to become one of the 20th century's most prominent couturiers, prevailing for nearly half a century.

If you have read Think and Grow Rich and watched the movie Coco avant Chanel it will be painfully obvious how Coco used the principles of Think and Grow Rich to build a massive fortune (and along with it, no doubt, a great life full of memorable experiences).

You see, successful people use the same principles, whether they know it or not.

As Napoleon Hill writes:

'TRULY, "thoughts are things," and powerful things at that, when they are mixed with definiteness of purpose, persistence, and a BURNING DESIRE for their translation into riches, or other material objects.'

Did Chanel have DEFINITENESS OF PURPOSE? Yes - she clearly wanted to create a statement in the world of fashion and change the way women dress. Chanel craved personal and financial independence, and was ruthless in her search for success. She was uni❑ue in revolutionizing the fashion industry with dress reform and in promoting the emancipation of women.

Did Chanel demonstrate PERSISTENCE? Definitely. There were long periods when Chanel was struggling to make ends meet, not knowing where she would find the money to pay the rent, or even her suppliers. But she never gave up.

Did Chanel have a BURNING DESIRE for riches? Chanel has been quoted as saying "I invented my life by taking for granted that everything I did not like would have a opposite, which I would like.". Chanel was born in a poor house and abandoned by her father. There is little doubt that Chanel had a strong motivation to create the opposite of her life circumstances.

THE HOUSE CHANEL

Founded in 1910 by Gabrielle Bonhuer "Coco" Chanel, the small shop selling ladies headwear moved to the upmarket within a span of one year. The Fashion House Chanel took the fashion world by storm and surprise with their ever-famous Little Black Dress and Tweed Suit. Their fragrance brand 'No 5' was launched in 1921 that went on to become their signature brand. Later in 1970 Gabrielle Bonhuer "Coco" Chanel also introduced No-19 after her birthday. Chanel's another famous feather in the cap includes quilted fabric which also has a "secret" quilting pattern sewn at the back to keep the material's strength intact.

Gabrielle Bonhuer initiated and popularized new designs and revolutionized the fashion world by going back to basics - which highlighted elegance, class, and originality. Popularly was known as Coco Chanel was at the helm as a 'Chief Designer' until her death on January 10, 1971. Died with her designer shoes on.

Coco Chanel, also famous for their hats were made famous when worn by fresh actors and the fashion divas across the world. About their line of jersies is is said that Coco Chanel changed women's relationships with their bodies as well as body language and attitude. Their jerseys showered immediate success, and the brand continued to become stronger.

Coco Chanel has always preferred and promoted authentic and comfortable lines. Be it for clothes or costume jewelery. They revolutionized the jewelery sceme when they launched themselves into jewelery market around 1924 and changed the jewelry concept and gained immese popularity that took them to new heights. Their jewelery was considered "the most revolutionary designs of the time."

In 1957 The fashion world applauded her as the 'most influential designer of the twentieth century'. She died in 1971 ending an era of revolutionary fashion. Her influence, however, did not pass with her death. Posthumous Assignments came to the fore some years later. In 1974, the House of Chanel launched eau de toilette which was in progress when Coco Chanel was alive. In 1978 the first non-couture- ready to wear clothes line was launched. In 1981 Coco Chanel launched their first eau de toilette range for men.

In 1983 Karl Lagerfeld was the new name attached to the fashion house He was the Artistic Director for Coco Chanel Fashion. He carried the Coco Chanel's legacy forward by surprising, revolutionizing and shocking the fashion world. But this time by changing Chanel's fashion lines from the now-predictable styles to funky cuts and eye-catching designs. And the fashion house has not looked back ever. Fragrance Coco was launched in Coco's honor. Fragrance for men, fine jewelry, unisex watches, skin care line.. they have been offering something new to the industry non stop. Chanel, boutiques, their logo everything is a topic of discussion for fashion lovers and critiques alike.

The latest revolution being the the Luxury Line, introduced in 2006 feauturing a metal chain embedded in leather bags. It's one of the most desired "it" bags for the moment

CHAPTER 4- THE INVENTIONS OF COCO CHANEL THAT CHANGED THE FASHION WORLD

Scroll through Instagram and it's highly likely that you'll come across a pithy quote from Gabrielle Bonheur "Coco" Chanel, posted daily by everyone from a 14 year-old vaguely fashion-conscious teen to an international style editor or blogger. Whether it's "Simplicity is the keynote of all elegance" or "Fashion fades, only style remains the same," Coco Chanel's legacy lives on not only through the leading luxury fashion house she founded ,but also her eternally relevant comments about style.

The interlocking Cs remain one of the ultimate status symbols and Coco's bobbed hair, bright red lips and forthright manner broke the mould, as she revolutionised women's fashion in the early 20th century. We look at just some of the ways in which the non-conformist, legendary designer was such a pioneer.

THE LITTLE BLACK DRESS

The women's wardrobe staple that is the Little Black Dress originates from a Coco Chanel design from 1926, which appeared as an illustration in American Vogue. Vogue editors christened the 'Ford' dress after the era's classic black car, asserting that the chic, long-sleeved design in unlined crèpe de chine would "become sort of a uniform for all women of taste." And weren't they right.

The innovative dress was a radical update for the modern women, revolutionary for both its striking silhouette and dark tone; since the Victorian times black had been associated with mourning. However, for

Coco, black was the epitome of simple elegance and always one to subvert tradition, she was the key proponent in making black a colour that could be worn every day. Rival couturier Paul Poiret reportedly scoffed at Chanel in the street, mockingly asking her, "What are you in mourning for, Mademoiselle?" The quick-witted designer responded, "For you, dear Monsieur." Touché!

TROUSERS FOR WOMEN

When WWI broke out in 1914, though women who worked within the public sector continued to wear skirts, many women who took on more manuel roles began to wear trousers and overalls in the workplace. Coco Chanel loved wearing trousers herself, often borrowing her boyfriend's suits, and she began designing trousers for women to wear while doing sports and other activities. Soon trousers became a fashion choice for women rather than merely a functional garment.

THE INTRODUCTION OF JERSEY

When Coco Chanel opened her first shop in Paris, a large number of the garments were made of jersey. Accustomed to silks, satins and other luxury materials, many of Chanel's customers were shocked by her choice of a fabric traditionally used for men's underwear. However, the innovative designer saw the potential for womenswear with the fabric as it wasn't expensive, draped well and suited her clientele's increasingly busy and active lifestyle. "I make fashion women can live in, breath in, feel comfortable in and look younger in," Chanel asserted.

THE 2.55 HANDBAG

In the 1920s, Coco Chanel grew tired of carrying her handbags in her hand and decided to design a bag that liberated her arms. Inspired by the straps found on soldiers' bags she added thin straps and introduced the predecessor to the 2.55 bag in 1929. When Coco returned to fashion in the mid-50s, she updated her design, creating the iconic 2.55 named after the date it was born, February 1955.

THE BRAID-TRIMMED BOUCLE COLLARLESS JACKET

Marie-Helene Arnaud, the Allure of Chanel, shot by Sante Forlan, 1958

The Chanel bouclé (buckled tweed) jacket is undoubtedly one of fashion's most elegant and most timeless pieces. Created in 1954 by the then 71-year-old Coco Chanel, the jacket was designed to free women from the constraints of the cinched-in silhouettes of the Fifties.

DESIGNER PERFUME

In an interview in the early 1950s Marilyn Monroe famously said: "What do I wear to bed? Why, Chanel No. 5 of course," and within days sales of the perfume skyrocketed. The fragrance was born some 30 years earlier when Coco Chanel met the Russian émigré, Grand Duke Dmitri Pavlovich who introduced her to a Russian perfumer, Ernest Beaux. After month's of arduous experimentation, Beaux presented Coco with ten samples of perfume. Coco chose the sample No. 5 and when asked why she responded: "I always launch my collection on the 5th day of the 5th months, so the number 5 seems to bring me luck – therefore, I will name it No. 5."

It was the first man-made perfume, using synthetic compounds rather than essential oils. Introduced in May (naturally) 1921, Chanel No. 5 is still the best-selling perfume in the world.

COSTUME JEWELLERY AND FAUX PEARLS

Coco Chanel by Lipnitzki, 1936

Coco Chanel greatly popularised the use of faux jewellery, bringing everyday, less expensive pieces into the mainstream with gold and fake pearls. Made from chains, beads and glass that were designed to be worn with casual daywear, Coco reasoned that women should be able to buy more affordable jewellery to accessorize with every day, rather than only possessing few, precious gemstones.

SAILOR TOPS

Coco Chanel by Robert Schall, Paris, 1938

Designed for functional purposes, the traditional cream and blue 'La Mariniere' became the official uniform of navy seamen in Brittany after the 1858 Act of France. Since then the Breton top has become one of the most stylish items, worn and adored by many of the world's most revered fashion icons such as Brigitte Bardot, Edie Sedgwick, Audrey Hepburn, Jane Birkin and Alexa Chung.

But it was of course Coco Chanel who made it such a coveted piece of clothing. Spotting it on sailors whilst on holiday on the French Riviera, Coco made the stripes popular amongst her set and it heavily influenced her 1917 nautical collection.

THE CHANEL SUIT

Coco Chanel in her atelier fitting actress Romy Schneider in the 1960s

On the 5th August 1923 Coco Chanel invited a small group of journalists to her salon at 31 Rue Cambon to unveil her new collection, which included the first Chanel suit. The editors were underwhelmed by it and the tweed twinset barely got a mention in reviews.

In 1939 when WWII broke out, Coco closed her shop and moved to Switzerland. Upon her return Paris and fashion in 1954, she reintroduced the Chanel suit as we now know it featuring a knee-length skirt, cardigan-style jacket, trimmed and decorated with black embroidery and gold-coloured buttons. This time around it was far better received and has become one of Coco's most iconic creations.

THE CHANEL TWO-TWO PUMP

In 1959 Coco introduced the two-tone spectator pump, a sleek beige chassis with a chic black toe-cap, inspired by men's sportswear as so many of her innovative designs were. Over fifty years later and the bi-coloured ballet flat is still one of the most elegant footwear choices for fashionable women across the world.

CHANEL'S PERFUMES- WHAT MAKES CHANEL SO DESIRABLE

Which woman would not want to own at least one bottle of Chanel perfume? House of Chanel the Parisian based fashion house is the most recognized name in the world of haute couture and had its beginnings in 1909 when Coco Chanel opened her first shop. Chanel at first sold only women's clothing such as blazers, skirts, sportswear and sweaters and in the 1920's Coco Chanel's haute couture revolutionized the world of fashion by her non fussy but elegant clothing.

It was only in 1921 that she stepped into the world of perfumes and created the now world famous and most popular of all perfumes Chanel No. 5. This was such a massive success that Chanel went on to expand her business which now includes shoes, bags, costume jeweler and many more fashion items.

After an eventful period in her life during World War II, which had nothing to do with Fashion or perfume, during which time she had to leave Paris, she returned in 1953 and discovered what could be called the other most famous house of fashion - Christian Dior, and by getting together with her former Chanel partner Pierre Wertheimer, she was able to bring into prominence the Chanel label once again.

Although Coco Chanel died in 1971, Alain Wertheimer, Pierre' son who took over the company in 1974 was able to secure the services of Karl Lagerfeld the designer and made Chanel No. 5 popular once again and with new perfumes being introduced regularly by the House of Chanel, her perfumes have gone from strength and have made a lasting impression in the fashion industry.

Let's now take a brief look at Chanel's famous perfumes, known the world over:

Chanel No. 5

Chanel No.5 the first and the most famous Chanel Perfume created in 1921 consists of ylang-ylang and a blend of florals such as Jasmin and Rose. It is said that Chanel No. 5 is sold at the rate of a bottle once in every thirty seconds!

Chanel Gardenia Perfume

Although originally created in 1925 and was a stunning illustration of his ability, Gardenia was reformulated in the 1980's and is completely different from its original. In spite of its name, the chief note of this perfume is not Gardenia, and is actually said to have notes of sweet tuberose, orange blossom and jasmine.

Coco Mademoiselle

Mademoiselle was launched in 2001 and has the pure sweetness and the inimitable style of Coca Chanel. It is a light and refreshing fragrance with understated elegance and carries overtones of orange and bergamot and middle notes of rose and jasmine finishing off with patchouli. Its bottle is similar to that of Chanel no. 5 and has a pearly white cap.

Allure for Women

A daytime perfume for women created in 1996 has a floral fragrance with notes of orange flowers, citrus, melons, peaches & plums.

Coco by Chanel

An evening wear perfume created in 1984 that has a blend of spicy and amber notes and is a complex mix of frangipani, mimosa, Bulgarian rose, Indian jasmine and French Angelica.

Chanel No. 19

Chanel No. 19 was created to personify Coco's characteristics of confidence, wit and femininity by her admirer in 1971 to celebrate her birthday on the 19th of August. This was a wonderful tribute to a woman, 87 years of age and contains notes of floral and green followed by May Roses and Irises and ends with subtle chypre and woody notes.

Une Fleur De Chanel

Coco Chanel's signature flower, the camellia which symbolizes elegance, style and femininity inspired this limited edition perfume that has a subtle, seductive fragrance.

Cristalle Perfume

A youthful fragrance for summer created by Chanel in 1974 ideal for daytime wear. This vibrant, feminine scent contains a blend of mandarin, lemon and pure citrus. It was relaunched in 1993 in a richer and concentrated floral blend as an Eau de Parfum.

Chanel perfumes are the ultimate word in glamor and fame with many celebrities using them including Hollywood stars who cannot do without it. Women all over the world would love to own even one bottle of Chanel perfume but hesitate due to its high price.

THE HISTORY OF THE LITTLE BLACK DRESS

The first little black dress was designed in 1920s, Paris, by Chanel and Jean Patou. It quickly became a "uniform for all women of taste," as Vogue magazine predicted at the time.

Before the 1920s, the color black was only worn in periods of mourning. Women who wore black were considered indecent or sinful. After the first world war, as well as the outbreak of Spanish Influenza, it became common in France to see women wearing black for long periods of time, and the stigma lifted somewhat.

A part of the "anti-corset" generation, Chanel invented much of women's style as we know it. She once described her work as "nothing more than transform[ing] men's clothing into women's jackets, haircuts, ties and cuffs." She worked hard to create clothes both simple and sophisticated, even if they created scandal.

Women were drawn to the dress by its simplicity, elegance and cost. A few years later, the Great Depression forced many people to economize, which increased the popularity of the little black dress as a cheap way to look smart.

Coco Chanel. Nettie Rosenstein, a New York-based designer, popularized the dress in the United States. Though some claim she invented the dress before Chanel, the evidence is slim. Elsa Schiaparelli, Chanel's rival, put her own fantastic twist on the LBD, by introducing a wrap-around version.

"Chanel's Ford," as the press then called it, had long sleeves. Subsequent decades have removed the sleeves and shortened the hemline. Perhaps the most famous little black dress was worn by Audrey Hepburn for "Breakfast at Tiffany's," not to mention the one worn by Betty Boop. Today, every style guide trumpets the dress as a wardrobe staple for all women.

And it's no wonder. The little black dress is practical, stylish, and looks good on people of all body types and skintones. It's slimming and doesn't draw attention to itself, making it perfect for showing off an accessory--or for eluding the male gaze. Edith Piaf, the "little black sparrow," wore simple black outfits so audiences would focus more on her singing than her appearance.

CHAPTER 5- THINGS YOU DID NOT KNOW ABOUT COCO CHANEL

Coco Chanel managed to create her own empire in a world ruled by men. She was their equal and sometimes she was even better than them. The non-conformist designer will always be one of the most influential figures in the fashion industry simply because she established the basic modern woman's look.

Here are the things you didn't know about coco chanel;

1. Coco Chanel got her start as a milliner, creating simple straw boaters devoid of the embellishments considered fashionable at the time. "The women I saw at the race wore enormous loaves on their heads, constructions made of feathers, and improvised with fruits and plumes; but worst of all, which appalled me, their hats did not fit on their heads," she once said.

In 1910, she opened her first shop at 21 Rue Cambon in Paris under the name Chanel Modes and began selling hats that would not only become the accessory style of the day.

2. Chanel No. 5 was one of the first fragrances to be named after a designer, and is said to be a tribute to Coco Chanel's lucky number. The story goes: In 1920, Chanel commissioned Ernest Beaux, a Russian-born Frenchman and former parfumier to the tsars in Russia, to create her debut perfume. After 10 months of work, Beaux laid out 10 different vials, numbered one to five and 20 to 24, for the couturier's review. She chose the fifth, perhaps on blind superstition. As she reportedly explained to Beaux at the time: "I present my dress collections on the fifth of May, the fifth month of the year, and so we will let this sample number five keep

the name it already has; it will bring good luck." And that it did. By 1929, Chanel No. 5 had become the best-selling perfume in the world, and, ultimately, one of the most timeless scents in history. To this day, a new bottle is apparently purchased every 30 seconds.

3. Among many famous Chanel-isms: "A woman needs ropes and ropes of pearls." But the designer herself would often wear a mixture of real and faux. In fact, the age of costume jewelry began with Chanel when, in the mid-1920s, she launched the first collection of its kind, featuring jewelry made from chains, beads, and glass, one that Harper's Bazaar dubbed "one of the most revolutionary designs of our time." Chanel is said to have felt that if women could buy jewelry more affordable than real pearls and gemstones, they could more easily accessorize. "Costume jewelry is not made to give women an aura of wealth," she once said, "but to make them beautiful."

4. When Chanel designed her first handbag, in 1929, she caused a minor scandal for including a shoulder strap, considered improper at the time. "I got fed up with holding my purses in my hands and losing them,"she said, "so I added a strap." Chanel later redesigned her iconic ▢uilted chain-strap bag, releasing it in February 1955. Hence its name, the 2.55.

5. When Chanel discovered knockoffs of her designs, she wasn't just okay with it, she supported it. The couturier came across accurate copies made with decidedly cheaper fabrics at low-end prices at S. Klein, a since-closed discount department store in New York City's Union S▢uare. Rather than bristling, she opted to capitalize on the advantages of prêt-à-porter and the free publicity that came with it. Upon returning home

to London, she staged a private runway presentation, noting on the invitations that guests were welcome not only to bring their dressmakers, but also to make sketches and take notes.

6. She is known all around the world as Coco Chanel, but this wasn't her original name. Born Gabrielle Chanel, she became "Coco" after being given the nickname by soldiers in the audience while singing on stage

7. Coco Chanel became very rich and famous during her life, but her childhood was a humble one. She was the daughter of a peasant and a street vendor and was born in a poorhouse.

8. After her mother died, she was sent to an orphanage in a convent, where she stayed until she was 18. It was here that Gabrielle learned to embroider, iron and sew.

9. Coco Chanel started her fashion career by designing hats. With the help of one of her male admirers, she opened her first shop in Paris in 1913. As it became more popular, she started selling clothes as well.

10. In the 1920s she introduced the Little Black Dress to fashion. Intended to be affordable and easy-to-wear, Vogue rightly predicted that it would be worn around the world.

11. Her influence wasn't just on clothes. At night, she appeared at the opera house with short hair, inspiring many women to adopt the new "garçon" (boyish) style.

12. Coco Chanel's revolutionary designs were elegant but also comfortable and practical, as they freed women from wearing corsets. She also dared to shorten skirts so that ankles could be seen!

13. In 1954, aged 71, Chanel reopened her fashion house after it had been closed for 15 years during the war. She told the actress Marlene Dietrich it was because she was "dying of boredom".

14. On 10 January 1971, after returning from a walk with her friend Claude Baillen, Coco Chanel died on her bed in the Hotel Ritz. Her last words to her maid Celine were, "You see, this is how you die."

15. .Nuns taught Coco Chanel everything she knows.

Coco learned the sewing trade from none other than the nuns who ran Aubazine Abbey, the orphanage she grew up in.

CHAPTER 6- CONCLUSION

It would be impossible to dispute the claim that Gabrielle "Coco" Chanel is the most famous designer in history — the reputation outstripping that of rivals such as Dior, Balenciaga and Yves Saint Laurent, all of whom gave much more to fashion than she did. Her great strength was her ability to read the times and the moods that changed them — and usually do so before anyone else did. She was a true catalyst for fashion change, but not always a very original creator.

Her story has become legendary and at least its basic facts are now part of fashion mythology, even to those who have no special interest in the fashion world. Biographies, memoirs, diaries, films, even a play; her life has been turned inside out for all to enjoy and there is no reason to believe that the flow of words and images devoted to her will diminish in the foreseeable future, any more than that intertwined Cs of the company's logo will ever go out of fashion.

Gabrielle Coco Chanel

Born in Saumur in a poor house hospice in 1883, Chanel was illegitimate. Her mother died when her daughter was 12, and any fortune teller would have predicted a dark and dreary life of sadness for her from that point. But anyone who could read character and willpower would have known the possibility of a different life path. Even as a young girl, she had beauty, which developed into a coquettish style that entranced men throughout her entire life, thereby enabling her to get whatever she wanted from them.

The facts of her early days are not easily verifiable. She grew up in a time — the last years of the 19th century — and in a place — rural France — when the lives of the poor were rarely fully documented. So, facts are scarce and, throughout her life, Chanel took advantage of this. She was good at self-mythologizing, and there was much to mythologise. As far as we know, she was christened Gabrielle and legitimised when her parents married a year after her birthday. She was one of five children and the family lived in abject poverty. When his wife died of tuberculosis, the father, an indigent pedlar, dumped his three daughters in the grounds of an orphanage and disappeared. Life in a strict catholic institution run by sadistic nuns, determined to bring all their charge to heel, had no such effect on Chanel except to make her rebel against all forms of discipline and fight to have her own way. They failed to break her spirit but certainly hardened her resolve to take control of her life as soon as she could.

Liberation came when Chanel went to Moulins to work as a seamstress and eked out a wage by singing in a bar, where she was nicknamed Coco after a song she sang. She was popular, not least because she had developed into a dramatically beautiful young woman. Her professional life began in 1906 when she became the mistress to a French textile heir and racehorse owner. fabric (and how she could use it) and horses were two of her life long passions, as were wealthy, influential men who paid the bills and helped her business endeavours. But being the mistress of a busy man was not enough for Chanel. Her ambition needed an outlet. So, her lover took the classic route out of a very common predicament of the time, and set her up as a milliner, not as a profession, but as something to pass the time. Everything changed when she met a handsome and wealthy Englishman who shared her equine passions. They fell in love, probably the only time Chanel ever did. He took her to Paris and, within a year, she opened her first millinery establishment in a narrow backstreet called rue Cambon, on January 1 1910. Her lover, Boy Capel, took her with him everywhere and she soon learned how aristocrats and the beau monde lived, talked and dressed. Chanel was not happy with the fussy, encumbering pre-world War I high fashion look and when Capel gave her a boutique in Deauville in 1913, she began an insidious private war to try to make women as modern and comfortable in their clothing as men were — especially active, outdoor types like Capel. In Deauville, she introduced casual knits and dresses shockingly simple compared to what was coming out of the salons of the couturiers in Paris.

She chose the right moment. The 1914-1918 war was not a time for extravagance and the privations of war made women more receptive to simplicity then they might otherwise have been. Chanel was increasingly intrigued by the casual elegance of men's clothing, especially for wear in the country, and took many ideas from Capel's wardrobe, which were the basis for what was, by the end of the war a good business, with a Couture house registered in rue Cambon and a thriving establishment "pour le sport" in Biarritz. Both exemplified the principles that illuminated Coco Chanel's entire designing life: the luxury of simplicity; the insistence on perfection of workmanship and quality of materials and perhaps, her most lasting gift to fashion; the need for a fashionable woman to be slim and keep slim throughout her entire life.

Chanel's life and happiness — if she ever were happy — were torn apart by the death of Capel in a car accident in 1919. She later said that with his death she lost everything, but it could also be said that she gained a great deal. France, like Britain, was still in mourning for the young men lost in the carnage of the war. It has been calculated there was virtually no family in either country untouched by tragedy — and mourning filled the streets of Paris and London with women wearing black. Having no real family, Chanel had stood outside this very important moment for women. Capel's death — as violent and saddening as death in the trenches — made a bridge between her and the rest of her sex.

Despite her lack of formal education, Chanel had an intellectual acuity rare in fashion circles. She was aware that young women, looking at their mothers, destroyed by the loss of husbands and sons, felt it almost a compulsion to not fall in love. The independent garçonne was changing ideas of femininity and slim, sportive Chanel saw the signs before anyone else.

She never trusted men. She would take the money in exchange for her body and use it to preserve her independence. She chose lovers for their power and how it could help her. After Capel, there was the Grand Duke Dimitri of Russia and the Duke of Westminster and, during World War II, Haus Gunther von Dincklage, despite the fact that it was treason to consort with members of the occupying German force in Paris.

I believe her "little black dress" of the '20s was inspired by three things. Firstly Chanel recognised the need for post-war mourning — even for young women — but thought that it could be more chic than the traditional women's needs. Secondly, she wanted women to stop looking down–trodden and destroyed with grief. So she turned to formal menswear; the stiff white collar and starched cuffs made a chic declaration of masculine conformity and superiority. Add to this the grim memory of the nuns, whom she never ceased to hate in their black habits and white coifs, and the fact that spicing the black of a dress with white collar and cuffs perversely made an aristocrat into an indoor servant who served the tea and ran the bath water, and you have the sort of complex Rubik cube that so much of Chanel's fashion had.

As the century morphed into the '20s, Chanel was acknowledged as one of the great fashion leaders not only in Paris but across the globe. Her style and palette seems as modern today as it was then: chic and sportive during the day, based on crisp, flattering linearity and romantic at night. It is often forgotten that in the '20s and '30s, she created feminine evening dresses of lace that gave women as much authority as her day wear did.

She didn't have everything her own way, of course there were other important couturiers in Paris, not least Vionnet, Madame Grès and Lanvin and her two arch rivals, Patou in the '20s and Schiaparelli in the '30s. Guarding her own position, she did everything to denigrate them and their style. Patou had great success in America — already emerging as a crucially lucrative market for French fashion, and one well worth fighting for. Schiaparelli had a fairground boldness and wit, which grabbed the headlines every season, to Chanel's deep chagrin.

Edna Woolman Chase, editor-in-chief of American, French and British Vogue for over half a century, frequently had run-ins with Chanel over how many editorial pages were devoted to her and to Patou. She objected to her clothes being featured on the same spread as his and frequently threatened to cancel her advertising if she couldn't have her own way. But Chase was every bit as tough as Chanel and it was usually the couturier who had to back down. As she observed: "Chanel has the spirit of a Till Eulenspiegel...One could never be sure whether her mischief making was deliberate or unconscious." I think the judgement of history would be less ambivalent.

Chanel spent World War II holed up in the Ritz with her German officer, von Dinklage, having closed down her business in 1939. With the cessation of war, France was out to punish those who had collaborated with the German occupation force. It was considered expedient for Chanel to leave France and she was spirited away to Switzerland, with the agreement of Winston Churchill it has always been rumoured.

And there Coco Chanel's career could have stopped, and she would have still held the honoured place she does today. But, instead, she decided to make a comeback — a risky decision for an old woman no longer in sympathy with the current fashions. Known as one of the leading modernises and directional creators of fashion in the 20th century, she had also, in Chanel No. 5, given the world its best known and most popular fragrance. Gossip at the time said that it was No. 5 that forced her decision, as it was losing its pole position without the glamour of clothes and fashion shows to bolster sales. Others claimed that it was Chanel's personal hatred of homosexual designers who, in the '50s, dominated Paris couture. Although she admired and accepted Balenciaga as a great craftsman as well as creator, she saw Dior, Balmain and others as undoing all the work she had done to simplify and modernise women's dress. She was determined to stop their chauvinistic romanticism (as it seemed to her) making overdressed masculine trophies of the modern woman whom she had worked so hard to create as a powerful being, largely dependant of men.

Chanel presented her new collection on February 5, 1954. The French press, still unforgiving of her behaviour during the war, were lukewarm but the American and British press saw her soft, little suits as a breakthrough uniting chic and youth in a fresh accessible way. Chanel had pulled off a coup and a miracle. The Chanel suit is a standard garment in modern fashion, worn by teenagers as well as their grandmothers. And the miracle? She was 71 when she made her comeback. She died, alone, in 1971, aged 88, after a hard day's work. Since that time more words have been written about her than any other fashion designer of the 20th century.

THE CHANEL HOUSE

The House of Chanel simply called Chanel is a French fashion house. This venture has indeed revolutionalised the conventional attires like corsets. Unfussiness and grace are equally given due position for the entire designer wears from Chanel. Cardigan Jackets and Chanel suits are their signature outfits. In the beginning, Chanel was the most favorite of all the elites in France. Now, it has been picked by the elegant and wealthy crowd in London and Paris.

Since the launch of this enterprise, there had been two eras in terms of the leadership. The first one, of course is the Coco Chanel Era, which was from the year 1909 till her death in the year 1971. The second era was called as Karl Lagerfield era that continued the rich tradition of new and innovative fashion lines.

Chanel had a humble beginning. She was the mistress of a division officer Etienne Balsan. She made eye-catching hats and all the fashionable ladies gave orders to Chanel for more and more copies. Later she started a couture shop and navy jerseys were her masterpiece attires. She was absolutely modern in her approach to patterns, such that the hemlines of her jerseys made ladies' ankle noticeable.

During the World wars, her contribution to the ladies' dresses is commendable. Her practical designs stating that the ladies wear should be simple, light and quick to carry opened up a new era.

The financial basis of this empire was Chanel No. 5, the phenomenally successful perfume she introduced in 1922 with the help of Ernst Beaux, one of the most talented perfume creators in France. It has been said that the perfume got its name from the series of scents that Beaux created for Chanel to sample—she chose the fifth, a combination of jasmine and several other floral scents that was more complex and mysterious than the single-scented perfumes then on the market. That Chanel was the first major fashion designer to introduce a perfume and that she replaced the typical perfume packaging with a simple and sleek bottle also added to the scent's success. Unfortunately, her partnerships with businessmen Théophile Bader and Pierre Wertheimer, who promised to help her market her fragrance in exchange for a share of the profits, meant that she received only 10 percent of its royalties before World War II and only 2 percent afterward. Despite enacting a series of lawsuits, Chanel failed to regain control of her signature fragrance.

THE END